C000129018

Secondhand Boat

The legal aspects

Mandy Peters
F.Inst.L.Ex

Published by
The Royal Yachting Association
RYA House Ensign Way Hamble
Southampton SO31 4YA

Tel: 0844 556 9555
Fax: 0844 556 9516
Email: info@rya.org.uk
Web: www.rya.org.uk

© Mandy Peters 2010

RYA 2nd edition

Typesetting: Creativebyte
Proofreading and indexing: Alan Thatcher
Cover Design: Creativebyte
Cover Image: Sunseeker
Printed in China through: World Print

CONTENTS

INTRODUCTION

The purchase of a boat is probably one of the biggest investments the average owner will make in their life. Even a relatively modest cruiser capable of going offshore is likely to cost tens of thousands of pounds, while a boat large enough to cross an ocean in real comfort, with a few home luxuries aboard, will cost well over a hundred thousand pounds.

And yet for all the expense and risk involved, the legal side of buying a boat can be as simple as buying a newspaper.

The Merchant Shipping Act 1995 defines a 'ship' as 'including every description of vessel used in navigation'. Thus any boat is capable of being a ship, even down to the smallest sailing dinghy or powerboat. By the same token, any boat owned by a British National is capable of being a British ship, entitled to registration on one of the British Shipping Registers, and also to all the rights and liabilities attaching to registered British ships under the Merchant Shipping Acts.

Unlike buying a house, it is possible for a boat to pass through many hands, from one owner to another, without ever being registered, or without registration details being changed on each change of ownership. This is because a boat is a chattel, (i.e. personal property) rather than real property (like a house) and because boat registration is voluntary in the UK (unlike a motor vehicle where the Road Traffic Acts require every change of ownership to be notified to the Vehicle Licensing Authority).

The absence of formality does not in any way imply that the buyer of a boat does not obtain good title. Although the first owner buying a new boat should receive a Builder's Certificate and a receipted invoice* from the builder or dealer, in many cases with the passage of time these documents are mislaid and subsequent buyers will often (perhaps unwisely) take over the boat by a simple verbal agreement and no documentation.

Although a boat can be bought and sold without formality and used without being registered, this is definitely not recommended. The purchase and use of a boat is full of potentially expensive pitfalls for the uninitiated and experienced alike; the purpose of this book is to identify those pitfalls and guide the buyer on how to protect his investment and his peace of mind.

*Showing VAT if the builder/dealer is VAT registered.

1 THE CONTRACT

It is a common fallacy among non-lawyers that a contract needs to be in writing to be binding on either party to an agreement. In fact this is not the case except for the sale of 'real property' (i.e. land, or a house) where the Law of Property Act 1925 specifically requires contracts to be in writing. A simple conversation on the following lines:

A.   "I like the look of your boat, how much would you sell her for?"

B.   "She's yours for twenty thousand pounds"

A.   "All right, I'll buy her for twenty thousand pounds,"

is sufficient to create a binding contract or agreement (the words are interchangeable).

So far as the seller is concerned, the simpler the deal the better. His priority is to sell the boat and to receive the money for it as soon as possible and to extinguish his responsibilities for the care and upkeep of the boat.

For the buyer however, the results of a quick verbal agreement of that sort could be absolutely disastrous. Unless he can be sure that the boat and all the fittings are in good condition, that all VAT and taxes due on the boat have been paid, that there are no yard, marina or salvage bills outstanding, that all the equipment to be sold with the boat has been listed and agreed, that there are no outstanding mortgages or legal charges on the boat, that all co-owners agree to the sale, that the actual ownership of the boat will not pass to him before he has arranged full insurance cover, that the boat is Recreational Craft Directive compliant or exempt and that his purchase monies are secure, he could be making a very expensive mistake.

However, a methodical approach to buying the boat, leaving out any potentially expensive shortcuts, should ensure that most of these risks are minimised; the size of the investment obviously justifies a thoroughly cautious and even suspicious approach, unless both boat and seller are well known to the buyer. The normal order of events is as described in Appendix 9.

Buying through a broker

Even if you are buying a boat through a broker as opposed to buying directly from a private buyer, the principle of 'buyer beware'

still applies. The broker will be acting on behalf of his client, i.e. the seller, and not you, the buyer. Anyone can rent office space and start trading as a broker. It is in the buyer's interest to ensure that the broker is a member of the Association of Brokers and Yacht Agents (ABYA) and/or the Boat Retailers and Brokers Association (BRBA) (a group association within the British Marine Federation (BMF)); and operates a Client account (see chapter 8) and has Public Liability Insurance. In the case of the latter you may sue him in the event of failure to deliver the boat, disclose a marine mortgage, or return your deposit. In case of doubt over the broker's credentials a buyer may wish to appoint his own broker or solicitor to act on his behalf during the purchase. The ABYA/BRBA will point you in the direction of a reputable broker in your area. Alternatively the RYA can advise on the choice of a specialist solicitor.

Buying direct

For buyers not buying through a broker or a solicitor, the starting point will be one of the standard form contracts available either from the broker (if one is involved in selling the boat), or from the Royal Yachting Association (reproduced in Appendix 1).

Bearing in mind the risk of entering into a binding agreement by a verbal offer and acceptance, the careful buyer will ensure that no commitment is made on his part until he has satisfied himself on every aspect of the purchase.

> Having found the boat of his choice, and before negotiating the price, he should make it clear to the seller that, if an offer is made, it will be subject to a written contract being entered into. Where the buyer intends to enter into a face to face bargaining session, it would be advisable to have two copies of the standard form contract ready to hand, so that the session can finish with both parties signing the contract and being bound by its terms.

Once the price has been settled, the precise terms of the inventory agreed, and all other points fully understood by both parties, the relevant parts of the written contract should be completed, and the documents signed, with each party taking a copy for his own use.

The standard form contract is printed in full at Appendix 1; it is important that both parties understand fully the matters that are dealt with in the contract, and the way in which the transaction proceeds under the terms of the contract. The contractual terms are laid out in the following sequence.

Parties

It may seem an obvious point, but both the seller and the buyer need to be sure exactly who is buying and who is selling the boat. It is important that any joint owner of the seller is disclosed, and if the boat is to be bought in the name of another person (or company) this should be written into the contract. Also, if the boat is registered in the name of a company (even a single shareholder company) it is essential that the sale is dealt with as a sale by the company, not the individual shareholder on a personal basis.

Purchase price and deposit

The conventional deposit is 10% of the agreed purchase price but there is no reason why the buyer should not offer a lesser sum and amend the contract accordingly.

In fact there is a good argument for limiting the deposit to an amount sufficient to cover the cost of hauling out and relaunching the boat for a survey, replacing any antifouling, fittings and furnishings disturbed by the buyer's surveyor, and any other relevant costs.

Experience has shown that in some cases the seller or his agent has been reluctant to repay the deposit where the buyer, in accordance with Clause 5 of the contract, wishes to reject the boat after the surveyor has found material defects. The seller may claim that the alleged material defects are too trivial to allow the buyer to withdraw and refuse to refund the deposit, giving the buyer no option but to resort to legal proceedings.

The purchase price, once agreed, is of course binding on both parties unless the buyer is able to rely on Clause 5 of the contract (defects disclosed by survey) to offer a lower sum. In that case it is for the seller to decide whether to accept or reject the lower offer.

Agreement for sale

The vendor's agreement to sell carries the legal implication that he has the right to sell, and that the boat is free of any encumbrances, charges, liens etc. This is referred to in more detail in Clause 3.2 and is also enforceable under Section 12 of the Sale of Goods Act 1979. Advice on checking the vendor's title is given in Chapter 4.

The boat and equipment

It may be that the seller wishes to retain the name for his next boat. If the boat is on Part I of the Register (see Chapter 3) the requirement for a unique name means that the buyer will have to contract to change the name of the boat after completion.

It is important for the buyer to make an inventory of the machinery, equipment and gear as early as possible in the transaction, as loose items worth many hundreds, even thousands of pounds, have a habit of walking once a price has been agreed. The inventory forms part of the contract and should be initialled by both parties after a joint inspection.

Value Added Tax and other dues

As EU VAT rules mean that EU residents should only use a boat within the EU if it is VAT paid or 'deemed' VAT paid, it is important to ascertain the VAT status of the boat early on in the transaction and to ensure the VAT status of the boat forms part of the contract.

Sea-trial/Inspection & survey

A sea-trial is considered desirable as the handling of boats can differ vastly and it is important for the buyer to experience how the boat handles. Pursuant to the contract if the boat does not perform to the buyer's satisfaction he has the option of withdrawing from the purchase.

A survey is considered essential by most owners, and the contract is designed to provide a period between signing of the contract and completion for the survey to take place. Typically the buyer will ask for 21 days to arrange a survey, but where both parties are keen to complete the transaction quickly, a surveyor may be instructed at a few days' notice and requested to prepare a written report immediately after the survey. This need only take 2 or 3 days, depending on the availability of an appropriately experienced and qualified professional. Further advice on surveys is given in Chapter 2. It should be noted that all expenses involved in a survey, including yard fees and preparing the boat for survey, are met by the buyer.

Notice of defects/acceptance of boat

The survey may disclose material defects that had not previously been seen on the buyer's inspection. This will give the buyer the opportunity to reject the boat, cancel the contract and claim his deposit back, or propose to the seller a lower price or the opportunity for the seller to remedy the defects. The seller of course has the right to reject a lower offer or a notice to remedy the defects and to look for an alternative buyer. The contract provides a strict time framework for both the buyer and the seller to take action after the survey, and both should bear these time limits in mind at all times.

Often the parties are left arguing over what amounts to a material defect. It is open to the parties, at the pre-contract stage, to agree what they consider to be a material defect e.g. a specific type of defect such as osmosis, a value, or a percentage of the purchase price and to insert a clause to this effect into the contract.

Non-use by seller

There have been cases where a boat has been damaged whilst being used by the seller following completion of the buyer's survey but prior to completion of the sale. For this reason the contract curtails the seller's ability to use the boat after survey.

Completion of sale

The buyer is required to pay the balance of the agreed price within seven days of the acceptance of the boat.

If the boat is on Part I of the Register (see Chapter 3) the seller should hand over the ship's papers at this time. In addition to the Certificate of Registry and Bill of Sale these should ideally include the Builder's Certificate, the original or copy VAT invoice, all contracts and Bills of Sale tracing ownership of the boat from new to the present transaction, confirmation of RCD compliance or exemption and all equipment manuals and service records. In practice many sellers are unable to produce much in the way of paperwork, but a valid Certificate of Registry, Bill of Sale, and evidence of VAT status (see Chapter 5) and RCD information should be regarded as essential. If the boat is unregistered or on Part III of the Register, also known as the Small Ships Register (SSR) (see Chapter 3) evidence of VAT status or exemption, a simple Bill of Sale (Appendix 5), a Certificate of Registry and RCD information together with any other available documentation is essential.

Seller's right to assign title

See under *Agreement for Sale* above. However, even though the seller guarantees under this section that he has the right to sell, and that the boat is free from any charge, the checks outlined in Chapter 4 should still be carried out.

Free access after completion

A boat laid up ashore may have easy access at the time of the buyer's initial inspection, but by the time completion has taken place the boat may be blocked in by numerous other craft being laid up. Removal of the boat by the buyer's contractors can mean great additional expense as boats are shuffled around the yard to make space for the removal.

Warranties

This section underlines the importance of a survey in buying a boat from a private individual. **The Sale of Goods Act provisions on satisfactory quality and fitness for purpose do not apply to private sales** and the seller is under no duty to draw defects to the attention of the buyer. If the seller has made specific representations, statements, or promises about the boat, that is a different matter, but proving such statements in court on a misrepresentation case is likely to be very much more costly and time consuming than commissioning a professional survey.

Risk

It is important that the risk in the boat should not pass to the buyer until he has completed his insurance arrangements (see Chapter 9).

Default

The contract provides for the rights of each party in the event of a default by the other. One point which over-optimistic buyers often fail to realise until it is too late is that there is no provision in the contract for changes of mind. Once the contract is signed, unless the survey discloses previously unseen material defects and/or the boat does not perform to the buyer's satisfaction at sea-trial, the buyer is bound to proceed with the transaction or risk losing his deposit and any additional costs (including the shortfall in price offered by a later buyer) involved in a re-sale.

Non-Production of Documents

Whilst the law does not prescribe the documentation that should follow a boat sale, documentation is required to evidence compliance with certain legal requirements; such as the Recreational Craft Directive and the boat's VAT status. The contract therefore contains a schedule of documents which should usually be available, however it does envisage the need for the parties to amend the list. Clause 13 entitles the buyer to withdraw from the agreement where the seller is unable to produce the documentation listed in the schedule.

Dispute Resolution

If a dispute does arise, it is preferable for the parties to try to resolve the issue through negotiation and where that is not achievable through Alternative Dispute Resolution, such as mediation. The British

Marine Federation have arranged a mediation scheme (see Chapter 13 for more details). Legal proceedings should only be entered into after all other avenues of conciliation have been explored.

Entire agreement clause

This clause provides that no other written or verbal statements should be taken into account by either party in interpreting the contract. This does not prevent the buyer from taking legal action in respect of any misrepresentation by the seller by which he was persuaded to enter into the contract. A representation does not form part of the contract and is not affected by this clause.

Syndicate ownership

More and more recreational boaters are electing to share the ownership of their boat between a number of syndicate members. Such form of ownership can help to ease the burden of the cost of purchase and upkeep and allows the enjoyment of sailing to be shared between a group of like-minded people. Syndicate ownership of a boat may well be between family, friends or even strangers; whatever the constitution of the members it pays to enter into a written agreement setting out their rights and responsibilities. We have produced a template agreement for the syndicate ownership of a boat, which is reproduced at Appendix 2.

THE SURVEY

Provision is made in Clause 5 of the contract for the buyer to have the boat surveyed and to carry out a sea-trial. Although the boat may appear to be in excellent condition, and a survey may appear unnecessary, it is a sensible precaution to take. A surveyor will usually find sufficient hidden problems with the boat to enable the buyer to reduce his first offer by at least the equivalent of the surveyor's fees; in more serious cases he can detect signs of potentially disastrous defects, and in any event his report will provide some level of guarantee since he will be legally liable for the costs of remedying any defects that he has negligently missed.

The detailed instructions given to the surveyor are of importance. It may simply be that a hull condition survey is required, or a full survey to include rig, sails, engine and all other equipment aboard. If the engine or engines form a substantial part of the value of the boat, it will probably be worthwhile having a separate detailed engineer's report, which may include a sea-trial and full report on the boat's performance.

The surveyor should also be given a copy of the particulars of sale and asked to verify any technical aspects, or references to measurements or to the age of the boat, that are important to the buyer. Even if apparently precise details have been included in a broker's information sheet, most such sheets contain a declaration that the particulars do not form part of any contract, and that buyers should check the accuracy of any statements for themselves.

Once the survey and engineers report (if any) have been received, the contract allows the buyer up to 14 days to decide on his next step. If the survey discloses no material defects, then the buyer is obliged to go ahead with the agreement. If on the other hand material defects are found which were not readily apparent on the buyer's initial inspection of the boat, he has the option either of withdrawing from the sale and having his deposit refunded, renegotiating the price to allow for repairs or renewals, or requesting the seller to rectify matters at his own expense prior to completion of the contract.

Whether a defect is material or not is a frequent source of dispute between the parties. Although there is no exact definition as to what is material, it could be said that if the cost of remedying the defect or defects is more than 5% of the agreed value of the boat then that is usually material, below that percentage it becomes more arguable according to the specific defect concerned. However, even an expensive defect may not be 'material' if it is a non-structural item that can be simply (albeit expensively) replaced.

When selecting a surveyor or engineer it is advisable to establish whether they have full professional indemnity insurance. The likelihood of a surveyor failing to detect a serious fault may be limited, but mistakes can be made and unless the surveyor carries insurance the buyer may find himself without financial redress. Most surveyors are members of a professional body such as the Royal Institution of Naval Architects or the Institute of Marine Engineers. There are however many who hold no formal qualifications but whose experience more than makes up for this. Membership of the Yacht Brokers, Designers and Surveyors Association (YBDSA) is limited to those with relevant qualifications or experience, and indeed the YBDSA insists on all its surveying members carrying full professional indemnity insurance.

In bygone days the majority of boats were built under Lloyds supervision, and this body still enjoys a worldwide reputation. However, in recent years a number of cases have arisen where the buyer of a boat with a Lloyds certificate has found to his cost that it does not provide a full guarantee and financial indemnity against defects. There is no substitute for the buyer instructing his own surveyor and having a report prepared for his own purposes. A report prepared for another person (e.g. a prospective buyer who has dropped out) may appear to cover all the buyer's points of concern, but it is unlikely that the buyer could take legal action against the surveyor for negligence since the report was not prepared for him, or on his own instructions. However in some cases the surveyor may agree (for a fee) to assign the survey to the buyer and be legally bound in respect of that previously prepared report.

If the buyer is electing to conduct a sea-trial, it would be usual practice for his surveyor and/or engineer to accompany him.

REGISTRATION

Boat registration in the UK is not compulsory unless it is intended to cruise outside of territorial waters. An owner may wish to register his craft for a number of different reasons, his reasons will dictate the form of registration he chooses.

Part I Registration

The Merchant Shipping Act 1995 provides for the registration of British-owned ships. Registration under Part I which is managed in Cardiff by the Registrar General of Shipping and Seamen, requires full details and proof of ownership to be provided by the applicant, together with a measurement survey report prepared by a qualified tonnage measurer. With measurement fee, certification fee, and the required marking of the vessel with the registered number, the total cost of registration is, at 2009 prices, in the region of £500, plus a five-yearly renewal fee of £49. However, since registration under Part I, in theory, provides the owner with evidence of title, it can make the later sale of the boat very much simpler, as a buyer need only satisfy himself that the seller is the registered owner, and the boat is not subject to a registered mortgage.

Part III Registration (Small Ships Register)

The SSR was instituted in 1983 in response to the requirement of a number of overseas authorities for British owned boats to be properly registered, and the reluctance of many boat owners to pay the full registration fee required. The SSR provides a boat owner going foreign with a Government issued document stating the name of the declared owner. The certificate is issued upon the completion of a form by the applicant (which nowadays can be done online) and is of no value as proof, or even evidence, of ownership. However, since the cost is £25 for a 5 year certificate and entitles the registered owner to wear a privileged ensign (provided he is a member of a relevant club) and to carry duty free stores (if taking his boat beyond the shores of the European Union), there are a great number of boat owners who opt for Small Ships Registration in preference to Part I Registration.

Checking the register

For the prospective buyer, checking the Register is the first and most obvious step that should be taken.

For a boat on Part I of the Register, the name and Port of Choice (or initials of the owner's club) should be marked on the stern, and the official number either carved in the main beam (at the deckhead adjacent to the main mast) of a wooden boat, or displayed on a plaque on the main bulkhead in the case of a grp or metal-hulled boat. The owner should also be able to show a certificate naming him as the registered owner. Having satisfied himself that the boat is the one referred to (including a check on the engine serial number) the buyer should then contact the Registrar General of Shipping and Seamen in Cardiff and request a transcript of the registration particulars. This transcript should contain all the information on the registration certificate, and in addition will also disclose whether any mortgage has been registered against the vessel. The buyer should beware however, since the Register does not allow for the reservation of title, in theory, it is possible for an unscrupulous seller to enter into a mortgage agreement with a finance house (or even sell the boat to another buyer) between the buyer's inspection of the Register and completion of the sale, particularly if there is a delay between the two. As a matter of practice however, the Registrar General's office, having provided a written transcript to an enquirer, will provide further information free of charge over the telephone to the enquirer up to a week after providing the transcript. The address and telephone number of the UK Ship Register is given at Appendix 7.

For boats on the Small Ships Register there is still some benefit in checking the registration particulars, as the limited information on the transcript may go towards building up a complete picture of the information provided by the seller.

Transfer of title

Once the buyer has completed his investigations of title and acted upon the results of the survey he will usually wish to go ahead with completion of the sale. Whether this is through a broker or privately he should not hand over the final balance of the purchase price unless he is given the relevant documentation to enable him to re-register the boat in his own name. In the case of a Part I registered boat, this will consist of the boat's registration certificate in the seller's name, and a Bill of Sale made out in the name of the buyer and signed by the registered owner (together with all other Bills of Sale in the seller's possession). If either of these is defective it will not be possible for the buyer to re-register the boat in his own name, and he will often be put to great trouble and expense in remedying the problem. If the seller is unable at the last minute to produce exactly the right documentation, then the buyer may either withdraw from the agreement in accordance with clause 13 of the contract or he may consider retaining a part of the purchase price (perhaps 5% or 10% of the total) against receipt of the required documentation.

It often happens for example that a seller did not take the trouble to re-register the boat in his own name when he originally acquired it. This does not signify that his beneficial ownership of the boat is in doubt, but it would involve the new buyer having to trace the original registered owner to persuade him to sign the Bill of Sale in his favour. If this proves impossible (as is often the case) the buyer will have either to wait until the current registration lapses before re-registering the boat in his own name, or make a formal application to the High Court for an order requiring the Registrar to transfer the title. These problems can be reduced by simple precautions at the time of completion.

Once the buyer has the Certificate of Registry and a Bill of Sale in his possession, these should be sent to the Registrar with the appropriate fee for change of particulars (£80 in 2009). An amended certificate will be sent back to the new owner in due course.

For boats on the Small Ships Register the procedure is very much simpler. Since the Register entry and certificate are not evidence of title, the only check that can be carried out is an inspection of the Certificate for any sight of obvious fraud and an enquiry to the UK Ship Register Office. Upon completion of the purchase of a boat on the Small Ships Register, the Register lapses and a buyer must re-register.

The cautious buyer will also carry out further checks as referred to in Chapter 4.

On completion of the sale the buyer should retain the signed contract, and obtain from the seller the original (or at the very least a copy of the) VAT receipt/invoice or other documentation evidencing the boat's VAT exemption status, a receipt for the money paid, a completed Bill of Sale which will help if kept with the ship's papers and produced as evidence of title when he comes to sell the boat on in due course, all other Bills of Sale in the seller's possession and documentary confirmation of the boat's RCD compliance.

4 CHECKING THE SELLER'S TITLE

As we have seen, there is no legal requirement for a boat owner to record his ownership on either of the official Registers. This obviously has implications for a buyer when purchasing a boat from a stranger, since in many cases he will not be sure that the seller has a bona fide right to sell, or that the boat does not have a loan outstanding against it, which could (and on rare occasions does) lead to it being repossessed by the finance company from the new owner.

Part I Registered Boats

For boats that are entered on Part I of the Register, the position is relatively simple. A buyer can satisfy himself that the boat is indeed the property of the alleged owner, and that there are no registered mortgages entered on the Register, simply by contacting the Registrar General of Shipping and Seamen in Cardiff and asking for a transcript of the Register entry for that boat. This is obtainable by post at a cost of £21. The transcript will show who the registered owner is, and for how long he has been the registered owner, as well as any registered mortgages (name of lender only, not the amount of the original mortgage nor the amount outstanding).

Liens

The buyer should however remember that although the entry on Part I of the Register indicates good title, and any unregistered mortgages are invalid against a bona fide purchaser without notice of them, it is still possible for other parties to have a lien or interest in the boat. Harbour Authorities, marinas, boat repair yards, crew, salvors (if the boat has been the subject of a salvage claim) victuallers, suppliers of equipment, and others, may all have a claim against the owner of a boat, in which case they may also be able to claim a lien against the boat itself, even when it has changed hands. This also extends to the VAT collection authorities if the boat is VAT unpaid (or if the owner cannot prove that there is no VAT liability). It is of course impossible for an intending buyer to be completely satisfied that there are no liens outstanding on the boat; the best he can do is ensure that the contract is signed (Clause 3.2 deals with liens, mortgages etc) and ask at the marina office, or the Harbour Master's Office if there are any known problems with the boat. Word of any unpaid bills, marina charges, harbour dues or salvage claims tends to circulate very fast, and the local grapevine is probably the best means of accessing this information.

Boats on Part III of the Register (Small Ships Register) or unregistered

The SSR was originally set up by the Department of Transport under the Merchant Shipping Act 1983 for the simple purpose of providing an inexpensive alternative to Part I Registration for boats going foreign. As we have seen (Chapter 3) registration of a boat on the SSR is a simple matter of the owner filling in an application form and forwarding it to the Registry of Shipping and Seamen, indeed owners may now apply for the SSR online. The Register is not intended to be a title register, or even to be evidence of ownership, and a registration certificate carries a warning to this effect; it acts as more of a passport enabling the boat to travel outside of UK territorial waters.

For boats registered on the SSR, or boats that are unregistered, there is no simple means by which a prospective buyer can check the seller's title, or check that there is no financial charge on the boat. Therefore, unless the seller and the boat are known to the buyer, it makes sense to investigate the title, even if the sale is through a reputable broker, since he is under no duty to run any checks on the seller's bona fides.

Ideally the seller should be able to produce documents of title showing the chain of ownership from the time the boat was built, down to the present time. These should include the original Builder's Certificate, the original/copy (receipted) VAT invoice from the builder, and subsequent signed forms of contract and Bills of Sale from the first owner to the second, and so on until the present owner. The seller may also be able to provide evidence of recent mooring charges, harbour dues, insurance premiums, maintenance and repair work or racing certificates; if these are consistent with what is known about the seller and the boat they will help to support the seller's contention that the boat is his to sell. Even if the seller is entirely lacking in any documentary evidence of his ownership, (and this is not unusual), he should still be able to refer the buyer to a yacht club officer, a Harbour Master, a river or canal authority, or a boatyard. Except in the case of the very smallest boats moved from place to place on a trailer, any seller who is unable to refer a buyer to someone reliable in authority or in the boating business should be treated with caution.

Checking on the absence of an unregistered mortgage is a rather more difficult matter. In the High Court case of *The Shizelle* (1992), it was held that an unregistered mortgage on an unregistered boat was valid not only against the original borrower, but also against any subsequent owner whether or not he knew of the mortgage. Given that a number of leading finance houses lend considerable sums of money on the basis of unregistered mortgages, this creates an obvious danger for buyers. In recent years a number of cases have occurred where a buyer in good faith has had his boat repossessed by the defaulting seller's finance house. In some cases this does not occur until months or years after the sale, and is usually triggered off by the seller missing one or more of his repayment instalments.

In the absence of any official documentation whatsoever the buyer needs at least to satisfy himself that the owner is who he says he is, lives where he says he does, and that the boat in question is the same vessel described in the contract. You may have to make enquiries as to where the boat has been kept, ask yards if they have ever done any work on her, and ascertain whether or not she owes any money. If the seller belongs to a sailing club then that is a good place to start. It is also advisable to check with the major marine finance houses (listed in Appendix 4) to confirm whether or not they have an interest in the boat in question. If you have employed a broker or solicitor yourself then you can safely leave this to him, and as a professional he will probably elicit more direct responses than you will as an unknown or lay person.

When all of the above has failed or is unavailable, a five year period must elapse before eligibility for Part I Registration is automatically assumed. Although SSR registration can be effected immediately you will be unable to re-register her in your own name on Part I. This may depress the value of the boat since buyers may be reluctant to take on a boat with no proof of title (which of course the SSR does not provide).

Boatmark scheme

In 1995, in response to instances of finance fraud, and also to discourage the theft of boats and boat equipment, the British Marine Federation set up the Boatmark scheme in collaboration with HPI Equifax. Unfortunately the scheme never really took off. It was hoped that all finance agreements on boats in the UK would be recorded and information made readily available to potential buyers. The Boatmark scheme is based on the Hull Identification Number introduced by the British Marine Federation in the mid 80s to provide every boat in the country with a unique identifying code number (now Craft Identification Number (CIN)). Each boat has its number clearly marked on the upper starboard corner of the transom, either during construction or at one of over a hundred marking stations around the country. This number becomes the key identifier for the record of that particular craft which Boatmark maintains in a database linked with the Police National Computer.

The boat's keeper receives a Certificate showing details of the boat, the date of first registration, and the name and address of the keeper. When the boat is sold prospective buyers are able to confirm the validity of the information on the Certificate by a simple phone enquiry and sellers have a ready means of demonstrating their boat's background.

At the time of writing (2009) the scheme is no longer being promoted by the BMF & HPI Equifax. Thus potential purchasers of SSR or unregistered boats are advised to carry out the checks outlined above.

Documentation

In so far as possible it is important when checking documentation to have sight of original copies.

5 VAT LIABILITIES

Value Added Tax was introduced in the United Kingdom in 1972, as a tax on the supply of services, and on the sale or import of goods. Any boats built in or imported into this country for private use since that date should be VAT-paid and ideally a seller of a boat should be in a position to provide the buyer with the boat's original VAT receipt/invoice, or at least a copy (ideally certified by the builder or original supplier as being a true copy). Unless the seller is able to produce evidence that VAT on the boat has been paid at some time, either in the United Kingdom or elsewhere in the EU, or documentary evidence that the boat is VAT exempt, the buyer may face a potential VAT assessment on the current value of the boat if an EU Customs official carries out a spot check.

Until the end of 1992 it was possible for a boat built in the UK, for a UK resident, to be exported immediately upon completion without payment of VAT, for use overseas on a tax-free basis. The International Convention on Temporary Importation provided that all convention countries should permit the free use of recreational equipment and 'means of transport' for touristic purposes for a minimum of six months in any one year. This rule was interpreted more liberally than the minimum in most European countries including France, Spain and Italy, and over the years tens of thousands of boats built for northern European owners enjoyed tax-free status in Mediterranean marinas.

The completion of the Single Financial Market on 1st January 1993 saw the end of concessions of this sort between EU States. Apart from a few months' grace for boats already enjoying tax-free status, any boat in any EU State, owned by a national of any EU State for his private use, must be VAT-paid. In theory it should make little difference which State the VAT is paid in, since rates are intended to be roughly equivalent (see Appendix 6 for details of 2009 rates). In practice however, experience has shown that some States tend to be considerably more flexible in agreeing modest valuations with owners, and allowing payments to be spread over an extended period. At the time of writing, the Customs authorities in the UK are not prepared to discuss valuations or payment terms unless a boat is actually within the UK (by which time it is obviously too late to negotiate). The importer of a boat from outside the EU may therefore find it to his advantage to import it first to another EU State where a valuation and payment terms have been agreed in advance (in writing) before bringing it into this country. Once a boat has been imported into any EU State and VAT paid, in theory no further VAT liability can arise within the EU. However it is important to note that if a boat is involved in a subsequent 'chargeable event' (i.e. retail sale/importation into the EU) a further VAT liability will arise. It is worth bearing in mind that if an EU VAT paid boat changes hands outside of the EU, she will lose her VAT paid status and VAT will be payable if she is re-imported into the EU.

The completion of the Single Financial Market on 1st January 1993 also saw the introduction of an amnesty for any boat in the EU area built on or before 31st December 1984. Therefore unless a boat owner in the EU is able to prove

either   that the boat is VAT paid
or   that it was in use as a pleasure craft prior to 1st January 1985
and *was in EU waters on 31/12/92 - 1/1/93,*

he is liable to pay VAT on the current value of the boat, and there may be spot checks in any EU State on any boat at any time.

The potential VAT liability is something that all intending buyers should be aware of. If the seller of the boat cannot produce full documentary evidence of her VAT status, the buyer may argue that the boat is worth only 100/117.5 of the asking price.

Further info is contained within HM Revenue & Customs Notice 8, 'Sailing your pleasure craft to and from the United Kingdom'. Appendix 8 contains an extract of Notice 8 dealing with deemed VAT paid status. A joint RYA HMRC VAT FAQs document is available to members from the Legal Team.

RECREATIONAL CRAFT DIRECTIVE

Most people will be aware that importing a boat from overseas will involve payment of VAT and Import Duties; but many are not aware of the requirement for the boat to comply with the Recreational Craft Directive. Lack of awareness of this requirement can prove to be extremely costly.

The purpose behind the RCD is to allow a single European market in recreational craft to operate.

Since 16th June 1998, all recreational craft with few exceptions, between 2.5 and 24 metres in length, sold or put into service in the European Economic Area (EEA) for the first time must comply with the essential safety requirements of the RCD, and must be CE marked to certify compliance. This includes imported boats either new or secondhand, and home built boats if placed on the market within five years of completion, which are intended for sports and leisure purposes. The builder, his agent, or the person importing the boat is responsible for compliance and marking.

The EEA includes all EU countries plus Iceland, Norway and Liechtenstein and EU overseas countries and territories. A list of EEA countries can be obtained from the Technical Department of the RYA.

A boat that comes within the scope of the RCD must have accompanying documentation. These include a Technical File and an Owner's Manual which must include a written Declaration of Conformity. The boat should also carry a CE compliance plaque in a prominent place.

The Amending Directive

The Amending Directive was introduced in order to allow a single European market in recreational craft to operate whilst maintaining a high level of environmental protection.

The Amending Directive (2004) applies to a wide variety of new recreational craft, including sail cruisers over a certain size, motor cruisers, motor boats and personal watercraft, whether powered by outboard, stern drive, or inboard engines. The changes also apply to existing craft and their engines that undergo major modification and conversions.

It introduced a further set of essential safety requirements, which include requirements as to emissions.

EU Member States were required to comply with most of its measures from 1st January 2005. However, there was a further transitional period to 1st January 2006 in relation to compression, four-stroke ignition engines and two-stroke ignition engines.

The RCD is enforced by Trading Standards Departments of Local Authorities. Breach of either of the Directives may result in a fine of up to a maximum of £5,000 and/or three months' imprisonment. It is therefore essential that the prospective buyer ascertains the boat's RCD status prior to entering into a contract with the seller.

A further RCD Directive has been approved which, when in force, will give more extensive powers to Trading Standards to enforce the requirements of the RCD. Points of entry may be monitored and it is envisaged that there will be a more joined up approach between Trading Standards and Port Authorities in order to help combat the so called 'grey imports' market.

For further detailed information on the RCD contact the RYA Technical Department on 0845 345 0383.

7 RAISING THE MONEY

Buyers may need to make arrangements to borrow the necessary funds from a bank, building society, finance house or some other source.

If the borrowing requirement is relatively modest (relative, that is, to the income of the buyer) and it is expected the debt will be cleared quickly, a simple bank overdraft will usually be the most convenient option. If it is likely to take the buyer more than 12 months to pay the loan off, for amounts up to about £5000, a bank will usually try to sell a personal loan plan; for larger sums a variable or fixed rate loan linked to the bank's base rate or finance house base rate (FHBR) will be offered.

High street banks do not normally take mortgages over privately owned boats, partly because the technicalities of registering a marine mortgage are outside their normal experience, and partly because of the high cost of formal registration with the UK Ship Register and formal notification of the mortgage. For sums in excess of about £25,000 however, they may well look for a first or second charge over the borrower's house. Rates may be negotiable.

Loans can be obtained from building societies against the borrower's (buyer's) property to finance the purchase of the boat. However the buyer should be aware that the building society's security is his home as opposed to his boat and his home may therefore be at risk if the repayments are not kept up.

The main players in the market are the specialist finance houses of which Lombard Marine Finance, Barclays Marine Finance, Bank of Scotland Marine and HSBC Marine Finance are still the leaders, but with a number of other lenders who are often able to provide attractive deals.

The advantage of dealing with a specialist house is the availability of specific plans for marine finance and staff who are solely engaged in that area of business. When dealing with loans of £25,000 or more, the finance houses will generally take a mortgage over the boat. The additional security provided by a marine mortgage will enable them to offer an interest rate comparing favourably with a bank's unsecured loan rate. When lending £75,000 or more the finance house will usually insist on the boat being registered on Part I of the the British Register in order to register their own interest. Their terms may vary.

Marine mortgage

Money has been raised on the security of ships for as long as there have been shipping and banking industries. The traditional method of mortgaging a ship (and the legal definition of ship includes "every description of vessel used in navigation") is by way of a formal charge on the Register of British Ships established under Part I of the 1995 Merchant Shipping Act. One of the main reasons for registering a boat under Part I of the Register, rather than the simpler and cheaper Small Ships Register, is to provide the basis for a formal mortgage to be arranged. No mortgage recording facility exists on the Small Ships Register.

The effect of a marine mortgage in favour of a financial institution is not to transfer ownership to the lender, but simply to restrict the borrower to using the boat in a way that will not prejudice the lender's security. Thus the mortgage agreement will usually include clauses about chartering, lending, parting with possession, part sales of shares in the boat, and of course insurance. In the case of a default in mortgage repayments the agreement will invariably allow the lender to repossess the boat without any of the formalities, or protective provisions, that the owner of a private house may be entitled to.

Where a borrower finds himself in difficulty meeting his repayments a finance house will attempt to reach agreement with him over a revised payment schedule. However if the borrower is unable to meet the (revised) repayment schedule and so defaults on the mortgage, even where repossession has taken place the law, as a last resort, provides the borrower with an equitable right to redeem the security by paying off what is owing. In such a case the court will make an order directing that the accounts between parties should be finalised and that if the mortgagor fails to pay the sum due within a certain period (normally six months) then the mortgage will be foreclosed and the mortgagee (lender) will become the absolute owner of the property.

Unregistered mortgages

As we have seen, boats registered on the Small Ships Register are not capable of being mortgaged under the procedures in the Merchant Shipping Acts. Although most financial institutions, particularly in the case of large mortgages on high value boats, will insist on full Part I Registration and recording of a statutory mortgage, a number offer an unregistered mortgage facility to borrowers with very much less formality involved.

This form of unregistered mortgage is intended to provide the lender with a comparable degree of security to that provided under Part I of the Register. Apart from the obvious cost advantage (the requirement for Part I Registration would cost the borrower in the region of £500 in addition to the £84 mortgage registration fee, compared with a £25 registration fee for the Small Ships Register), an unregistered mortgage works in such a way as to vest actual title in the boat to the lender.

Repaying the mortgage

Although most finance houses are happy to allow terms of up to 5 years for cheaper craft, or up to 15 years at the top end of the market, some may attach penalties to mortgage agreements to discourage early settlement. Since this policy varies from one finance house to another, it will be worthwhile including this point when comparing rates from one company to another.

PROTECTING YOUR PURCHASE MONIES

There have been a number of high profile dealer and broker failures within the industry and this has understandably caused some concern with buyers over the security of their purchase monies. Whilst it is fair to say that 99.9% of boat purchases go through without any hitches, the prudent buyer will nevertheless wish to ensure that his purchase monies are protected.

Protecting your monies when using a broker

If you are using a broker you should ensure that the brokerage is a member of either the ABYA and/or the BRBA; members of these organisations must adhere to the Associations' Code of Practice/ Code of Conduct which regulates the manner in which the broker deals with his customers.

You should also ensure that the brokerage operates a properly administered designated client account; this is an account in which client monies are held by a brokerage and which should be kept completely separate from the brokerage's current account. The use of a client account *should* provide better protection for client monies in the case of the brokerage getting into financial difficulties and becoming insolvent.

Operating a client account became a requirement for BMF/BRBA members involved in brokerage from July 2008. Members must provide evidence that their bank confirms that it considers the client account to be completely separate from the company's current account or that the brokerage has an arrangement with a solicitor to hold client monies on behalf of clients during the brokerage transaction.

ABYA members are required to hold Professional Indemnity and Public Liability insurance and operate a client account.

If the broker is neither a member of ABYA and/or the BRBA and does not operate a properly administered designed client account you may wish to consider instructing a solicitor to hold the purchase monies in a solicitor's client account pending completion of the purchase.

Broker holding monies as stakeholder or agent

A broker may hold purchase monies on account as either the seller's agent or as stakeholder for the parties. From a buyer's point of view it is preferable for the broker to hold purchase monies as stakeholder for the parties as this means that the broker holds the monies on behalf of both parties and cannot release the money to either party without the consent of the other. The effect of this is that your monies are held safe in the broker's client account and should therefore be recoverable in the event of the seller defaulting on the transaction or indeed your withdrawal from the purchase in the circumstances provided for in the contract.

If the broker holds the purchase monies as agent for the seller he may hand over monies to the seller upon demand; this could be disadvantageous for buyers as it would mean that the seller may use the monies and the buyer may therefore have trouble trying to recover his purchase monies if the purchase should fall through either due to the default of the seller or in accordance with the provisions of the contract. Thus wherever possible a buyer will wish to ensure that the broker holds the monies as stakeholder for both parties.

Protecting your monies when dealing direct with the seller

Where you are purchasing a boat direct from a seller (with no broker involvement) it is usual for the seller to hold the deposit pending completion of the transaction. However, where the transaction has not proceeded to completion, this can and indeed has in the past led to disputes over the return of the deposit. The parties should therefore stipulate clearly within the Sale and Purchase Agreement under what circumstances the deposit is to be returned and whether there are to be any deductions from it.

To avoid any potential conflict, the parties may agree to use the services of a solicitor to hold the purchase monies on behalf of both parties (i.e. as stakeholder) in the solicitor's client account until completion or termination of the agreement.

The parties should agree that the day the purchase monies appear as cleared funds in the seller's bank account is the day that the buyer takes over legal title to and physical possession of the boat.

It has become common practice for the parties to make use of telegraphic transfers or BACS methods of payment of purchase monies. This has the benefit of being handled in a secure manner by the bank with the transfer of the funds taking place within a defined timescale. Historically sellers were willing to accept banker's drafts, however, because the status of a banker's draft may differ from finance house to finance house it is becoming a less common method of payment; although provided the parties understand exactly how the finance houses involved in the transaction operate their banker's draft system then there is no reason why one should not be used.

INSURANCE

Although insurance for pleasure boats in this country is not yet compulsory, there is so much scope for damage to the boat, the crew, or other vessels in the ordinary course of navigation that it would be foolish not to have comprehensive insurance cover.

Unlike the simple form of contract used in household and motor car insurance, the standard boat insurance policy is a complex document. It is difficult for the layman to understand the contract fully without access to the Marine Insurance Act 1906 and the body of marine insurance case law contained in the Lloyds law reports.

The boat insurance market is highly competitive, divided between a number of Lloyds underwriters (who may be approached either through an agency or via Lloyds brokers) and insurance companies (who may be approached either through Lloyds or non-Lloyds brokers or direct). In the insurance market as anywhere else you get what you pay for, and while it is wise to shop around you should not be tempted to go for the underwriter or company offering the lowest premium for that reason alone. Experience has shown that underwriters and companies away from the cheaper end of the market tend to be more flexible in interpreting the strict terms of the policy in the case of difficult claims, and speedier in settling the more straightforward ones.

Also, since the 1994 European Directive on Unfair Terms in Consumer Contracts came into effect, most UK insurers have introduced new policy wordings to comply with the rule that contract wordings should be drafted in plain intelligible language. While this is to be generally welcomed, as the old Lloyds Institute Yacht Clauses were difficult to interpret, this approach has given rise to a wide variety of policy conditions, and while one insurer's cover may seem very much less expensive than another's, it may be that a close and expert comparison of the policy document will show the cheaper company to be offering very much more limited cover.

When a broker is approached for a quotation, he will usually quote a premium based on a number of underwritten features of the declared value of the craft. There is always room for negotiation over premium rates, as the nature of risk varies according to a number of factors. Is the mooring secure against extremes of weather? Is the area patrolled by police or harbour officials to discourage vandalism and theft? What is the intended cruising range? Does the owner have any qualifications? Has the craft been built to current standards (and does the insurer regard that as relevant)? Is the owner prepared to carry a reasonable excess? Is the owner a member of a club that entitles him to a discount?

Most underwriters will be happy to insure a boat up to 20 years old, without a survey being required. For older boats a survey is usually required, and it will normally be a condition that the surveyor's major recommendations be implemented before full cover is given.

It is essential when completing the proposal form to put in the fullest and most accurate information and to answer all the questions literally. The proposal form constitutes the basis of a binding contract, and in the event of a claim, most underwriters will re-examine the proposal to ensure that the claim is valid within its terms of reference. The law recognises that insurance contracts are one-sided; the boatowner knows everything about himself, his boat and the nature of his proposed use of the boat. Since the insurer only knows what the owner chooses to tell him, he is protected by the principle of uberrima fides. Roughly translated this means that the insured must show the 'utmost good faith' in providing information, failure to do so will entitle the insurer to avoid the contract even if a subsequent claim is entirely irrelevant to the subject matter of the false statement.

So far as the average UK-based boatowner is concerned, there are three main cruising ranges available at standard prices which must be declared on a proposal form, these are:

(a)   non-tidal waters within the UK;

(b)   coastal cruising within an agreed range;

(c)   full coastal and sea-going cruising within the 'home trade' limits, which cover all UK waters and continental coasts from Brest to Elbe, (some policies may include continental inland waters as far south as Paris. Most specialist boat insurers can provide wider cruising areas, for example, inland Europe, Mediterranean and beyond.

Particularly in the case of fast motorboats (insurers normally attach special conditions to boats capable of 17 knots or more) security against theft, or against the weather while at a mooring or at anchor is a major concern to insurers. They will usually insist that if a trailed boat is not kept at home, it must be made secure in a locked compound, and if left afloat unattended, must at all times be on a secure and reasonably sheltered mooring with some form of anti-theft device.

Unlike motor insurance, where the value of a car in the event of a write-off is taken to be its current market value, marine insurance policies are based on either a) the principle of agreed value; if a boat is insured for, say, £10,000, and in the case of total loss the insurers are able to show that it would have fetched no more than £8000 on the open market, they are still liable to pay the full figure. Provided the insured has not deliberately over stated the value, there should be no argument on the matter. This does not of course exempt him from accurately stating the price paid on the proposal form; this is not necessarily the same as the value of the boat, although insurers may wish to know the reason for any difference in these figures; or b) market value which provides insurers with the power to negotiate on value once it has been agreed that the claim is recoverable. It is important to establish on which basis you are insuring your boat.

Underwriters will of course need to be informed of any intention to use the boat for charter, whether bareboat or skippered, or for any commercial purpose. While this is not a problem in itself, underwriters will normally lay down conditions about the qualifications and experience of prospective charterers. For example, insurers will require charter vessels to comply with the MCA Small Commercial Vessel Code of Practice.

Under the speedboat clauses in most policies, any use for racing or speed trials is specifically excluded, and special insurance should be taken out with the club organising any such event. In relation to yachts, loss or damage to the rig is usually excluded whilst racing. Such cover can be negotiated upon the payment of an additional premium on the replacement value dependent on the type of racing.

Difficulties can arise when an owner forgets to lay up (or re-launch) his boat on the date stated on the proposal form. Claims have been turned down by underwriters on the grounds that the nature of risks while afloat are very different to those ashore. While most insurers are flexible about varying lay-up and relaunch dates, it is wise to inform them in advance of any proposed variation.

Most policies will provide cover, in an appropriate sum, for salvage fees or wreck removal, although it is advisable to check.

So far as third party liability is concerned with effect from May 2004, most standard policies provide the owner with indemnity up to £2 or £3m. The RYA recommend a bare minimum of £2m. It should be remembered that such a high figure will rarely be approached, even in the case of a bad accident, as the Merchant Shipping Act Limitation of Liability provisions will normally apply. The effect of the limitation provisions is to allow a boat owner (or his insurers) to limit liability for third-party property damage to approximately £500,000, and for death or personal injury to approximately 1 million; (the rate is subject to change). However, since limitation does not always apply in every circumstance, it is as well to carry substantial insurance against such misfortune.

It is advisable to purchase liability cover for water skiers and other types of towed beach toys as an addition to the boat policy as this type of cover is usually excluded from most standard policies.

An increasing number of harbour boards and navigation authorities are imposing third-party insurance requirements, this trend is likely to continue. In this context an important aspect of the cover provided is the cost of raising and removing the wreck of an insured boat in the event of it sinking in the fairway of a harbour or in the main channel of a navigable river or canal.

Some countries have compulsory insurance requirements and your insurer should be able to provide you with the appropriate documentation to satisfy the insurance requirements of the countries you intend visiting. Higher premiums will be payable on boats taken to overseas territories.

FINDING A MOORING

In conjunction with the purchase of your boat you will need to consider where you intend to keep it. Moorings are one option and can be found in our creeks, estuaries, rivers, harbours and marinas. Some areas, particularly where there is a high concentration of boaters, undoubtedly have a shortage of moorings and they are consequently expensive; it therefore pays to shop around for a suitable place to park your boat. Alternatively you may wish to consider keeping your boat on a dry-stack (if suitable, e.g. a RIB) or even purchasing a trailer sailor that you can keep at home.

Owners wishing to keep their boats in a marina will find most of the available options contained within the RYA Marina Guide published annually and on the RYA website www.rya.org.uk

The Yacht Harbour Association (TYHA) is the association for the development of coastal and inland boating facilities; its membership includes marina and mooring operators. www.berthsearch.com has been set up by TYHA to assist boat owners in finding suitable berthing options in their required location.

The Yacht Harbour Association
Evegate Park Barn, Smeeth
Ashford, Kent TN25 6SX

Tel: 01303 814434
Fax: 01303 814364

www.yachtharbourassociation.com

The Crown owns a large part of the seabed up to the territorial limit of 12 miles, which is managed by the Crown Estates Commissioners. The Crown has over the years sold the rights to part of the foreshore and seabed to private landlords. It has also leased or licensed Harbour and Local Authorities to manage parts of the foreshore and seabed.

The Crown Estate
16 New Burlington Place
London W1S 2HX

Tel: 020 7851 5000

enquiries@thecrownestate.co.uk
www.thecrownstate.co.uk

You may wish to contact your local Harbour Authority and/or your Local Authority to ascertain the availability and cost of moorings in your area.

BUYING FOR USE ON INLAND WATERS

Although there have been construction and equipment regulations in force on the River Thames since the mid-1920's, regulations for privately-owned craft on waters controlled by British Waterways, the Norfolk and Suffolk Broads Authority and other Environment Agency waters (the Medway and Anglian rivers) are a relatively new concept, and will need to be complied with if it is intended to base a boat on those waters.

The two principal navigation authorities introduced a national Boat Safety Scheme (with effect from 1st January 1997) and have developed a training course and qualification scheme for inspectors. The intention is that a navigation licence or registration certificate will only be issued for craft that have a current certificate of compliance issued by an authorised inspector. If it is intended to base a boat on any BW or EA waters, compliance with the scheme will be compulsory.

Details of the scheme are available on request from:

British Waterways
64 Clarendon Road
WATFORD
WD17 1DA

Tel: 0845 671 5530
www.british-waterways.co.uk

Environment Agency
Recreation and Navigation
Rio House
Waterside Drive
Aztec West
Almondsbury
BRISTOL
BS12 4UD

Tel: 08708 506506
www.environment-agency.gov.uk

BUYING FOR COMMERCIAL USE

Reference has been made to regulations established by the Department for Transport for commercially-used pleasure craft. Most of the Merchant Shipping legislation laying down rules for the design, construction and equipment of ships specifically exempts pleasure yachts or pleasure craft from compliance. However the *Marques* incident in 1985, in which a converted trading schooner capsized and sank with serious loss of life in a Tall Ships Race, led to the DfT amending the rules to exclude commercially used boats from exemption, and to require them to comply with a stringent Code of Practice. The regulations have been in force since 1994.

Boats used bona fide for the private pleasure of an owner or his family or friends, or within a club syndicate, are exempt, provided that any contribution to costs is for running expenses only. Any charters, whether crewed or bare-boat, will bring a boat within the regulations, and indeed any other commercial purpose will also necessitate compliance with the Code of Practice.

The regulations cover various areas of operation, in 5 categories from less than 20 miles from a safe haven, to unrestricted service, and encompass all aspects of design and equipment, including stability requirements, weathertightness, requirement for diesel engine, detailed electrical arrangements, fire prevention requirements, and lifesaving and safety equipment.

Many of these requirements will certainly be expensive to comply with, and undoubtedly go far beyond what has conventionally been considered adequate for cruising boats in the past. Any prospective owner considering subsidising his costs by occasional chartering (let alone running the boat on a full-time charter basis) should study the Code of Practice in detail and draw up detailed costings of the additional construction and equipment requirements, before entering into a binding contract to buy the boat.

Details of the Code of Practice for craft up to 24 metres can be obtained from:

Maritime and Coastguard Agency
Spring Place, 105 Commercial Road
Southampton SO15 1EG

Tel: 023 8032 9100
www.mcga.gov.uk

RESOLVING DISPUTES

If you have followed the guidance in this publication you should have minimised the chances of things going wrong with the purchase of your boat. However the sad fact is that disputes do arise and it is useful to know the steps you can take to improve the chances of a dispute being settled in your favour.

Use the RYA Agreement for the Sale and Purchase of a Secondhand Boat or where appropriate one of the standard Brokerage contracts; the terms of which you should ensure you fully understand. If things do go wrong familiarise yourself with any legislation; you need to make sure you actually have a case before you start pursuing the matter in earnest.

Contact the other party by phone inviting him to put forward settlement proposals. If possible try to arrange a face to face meeting. Quite often a face to face meeting is all that is required to resolve any niggles that have been building up between the parties.

Once you have entered into the realms of there being a dispute you should back up all your meetings and telephone conversations with written confirmation of what was discussed.

Set up a timescale with the other party for responses, settlement proposals, meetings etc; this way you will know when you are being ignored and can then take the next appropriate steps without having wasted too much time waiting for non-existent responses to your correspondence.

If you are in dispute with a broker/trader who is a member of a Trading Association, you might wish to consider reporting the dispute to it and also to Trading Standards.

An expert report may also help to resolve a dispute. In some cases both parties may agree jointly to appoint an expert, often a marine surveyor, with the parties possibly agreeing to be bound by the expert's findings. At the very least an expert report may add weight to your case.

Mediation should be considered as an alternative method to legal proceedings to resolve the dispute. This process brings in an independent mediator who will try and help the parties reach a satisfactory settlement without resorting to court proceedings. Unlike court proceedings, the parties to a mediation play a pivotal role in the course of and outcome of the mediation. The mediation will usually take place fairly promptly and at a reasonable cost.

Should you get into a contractual dispute with a BMF member, the BMF recommends that the parties engage in some form of alternative dispute resolution before resorting to often costly and time consuming litigation. The Academy of Experts run a mediation scheme especially for BMF members to deal with marine disputes with customers and suppliers, however because the mediators are experts in the marine field the scheme is appropriate for use by anyone with a marine dispute. For further information on this scheme please visit
www.britishmarine.co.uk/mediation or contact BMF on 01784 473377.

Legal Copyright Notice

The RYA Legal Team produce information leaflets, standard templates, agreements and documents for use by members and affiliated clubs. This material is protected by copyright which is owned by the RYA.

USE:

- RYA members may use the material for non-commercial private purposes.

- Affiliated clubs may use the material for non-commercial purposes such as attracting and retaining members, regulating the affairs of the club and organising events for members and non-members.

The material produced by the Legal Department is not otherwise to be incorporated or distributed in any work or in any publication in any form without the permission of the RYA Legal Department.

MODIFICATION:

The standard documentation produced by the Legal Department is intended to be reasonably comprehensive but cannot cover all eventualities. It is therefore anticipated that, in many instances, RYA members/affiliated clubs will need to amend the documentation to meet specific requirements. Where members/affiliated clubs do amend RYA standard documentation they should make this clear on the documentation.

The agreements shown are updated from time to time, please contact RYA Legal Team Tel: 0845 345 0373 or visit www.rya.org.uk

APPENDIX I

AGREEMENT FOR THE SALE AND PURCHASE OF A SECONDHAND BOAT

An agreement prepared by the Royal Yachting Association for the sale of a secondhand boat between persons not normally engaged in the business of selling boats.

This document is intended to create a legally binding contract; any Party contemplating signature is advised to take appropriate independent advice before doing so.

AN AGREEMENT dated the………day of…………20…………..

BETWEEN:

1. 'The Seller(s)' : (Name)

     of   : (Address)

2. 'The Buyer(s)' : (Name)

     of   : (Address)

In respect of the boat described below:

Name of Boat:

Flag and Port of Registry (if any):

Lying at:

Register Status: (Part I/Part III/Other/Unregistered)

Official No: **HIN/CIN Number:**

Principal Dimensions:

Hull Length Overall: **Beam:**   **Draught:**

Gross registered Tonnage:

Engines (make, power and date of build):

Description and Construction Materials:

Builder:

Date of Build:

Date of Purchase by Seller:

Financed   YES/NO   By:

Amount of Finance Outstanding at Date of Agreement:

VAT Paid in EU?   YES/NO

1.   Agreement for Sale

The Seller agrees to sell and the Buyer agrees to buy the boat free from all mortgages, debts, claims and charges of any kind at all (subject to the conditions and terms of this Agreement), together with all her gear and equipment as set out in the inventory attached hereto and signed by the Parties, but not including provisions or the Seller's personal effects, for the Purchase Price.

The Parties are strongly advised to prepare, sign and attach to all copies of this Agreement a full inventory of equipment included in this sale.

1.1 The 'Purchase Price': £...sterling
(in words..)
The Deposit (if applicable): £...................................sterling
(in words..)

Although this Agreement is fully legally binding without a Deposit, either Party may prefer a Deposit to be paid (typically anything from 1% to 10%); the Seller to cover himself against sea-trial or haul-out charges or remedial work after survey or other wasted costs; the Buyer as a "comfort factor" that he has secured the boat. Where the Parties agree that no Deposit is required, all references to the Deposit (in italics throughout) should be deleted.

2.   Value Added Tax and Duties

The price is inclusive of all VAT or Customs Duty which may be payable by the Seller on the boat.

If the Price is not inclusive of VAT or any tax or duty, or original documentary evidence is not available, the Buyer should seek independent advice and other appropriate terms should be agreed and recorded regarding responsibility for their payment.

2.1 The Seller warrants that the boat has been properly imported into the EU and that all appropriate taxes and dues have been paid and all relevant regulations have been complied with.

If the boat has not been properly imported into the EU then the Buyer should be aware that importation into the EU will require payment of VAT and compliance with the Recreational Craft Directive.

2.2 *On the signing of this Agreement the Deposit is to be paid to the Seller.*

3. *Payment of Balance and* Completion of Sale

Upon acceptance of the boat by the Buyer in accordance with Clause 7, the Deposit shall be treated as part payment of the Purchase Price.

3.1 Within seven days of acceptance of the boat by the Buyer in accordance with Clause 7, the Buyer shall pay the balance of the Purchase Price including any Value Added Tax due thereon and the Seller shall:

3.1.1

In the case of a Part I registered boat

Provide the Buyer with the current Certificate of Registry made out in the Seller's name, together with all other documents relating to the boat as set out in the attached schedule and shall execute a Bill of Sale in the prescribed form in favour of the Buyer, showing the boat to be free of all liabilities and completed so as to ensure transfer on the Register;

OR

3.1.2

In the case of a Part III registered or unregistered boat

Provide the Buyer with a Bill of Sale in favour of the Buyer showing the boat is free of all liabilities, together with all other documents relating to the boat as set out in the attached schedule.

3.2 By delivery of the documents specified in either case the Seller shall be deemed to have covenanted AND HEREBY COVENANTS that he is the sole legal and beneficial owner and has the right to transfer property in the boat and that the same is free of any encumbrances, mortgages, charges, liabilities for duties, taxes, debts, liens and the like except those that are the responsibility of the Buyer under Clauses 5 and 7.2, or otherwise specifically stated in this Agreement.

3.3 Where payment is made by cheque, draft, letter of credit or other instrument, the terms of this agreement shall be deemed not to have been fulfilled until such payment is cleared into the payee's account, or paid to the Seller in cash or by Banker's Draft.

3.4 On completion, the Seller shall ensure that the boat is available for collection by the Buyer, and that free access by the Buyer together with all necessary haulage equipment is permitted at no additional cost to the Buyer.

4. Warranties

The Seller is not selling the boat in the course of a business, and the Buyer is free to inspect the boat and satisfy himself as to her condition and specification. Therefore all express or implied warranties or conditions, statutory or otherwise, are hereby excluded unless specifically included in this agreement, and the boat, her gear and equipment shall be taken with all defects and faults of description without any allowance or abatement whatsoever.

5. Sea-trial, Inspection and Survey

5.1 The Buyer shall be entitled to require the Seller to perform a sea-trial of the boat, her gear and machinery and all items included within the sale. The duration of such sea-trial shall be proportionate to the cost and complexity of the boat and its systems but, unless specifically agreed at the time of contract, shall not be shorter than 1 hour nor longer than 8 hours. The Seller shall be obliged to insure the boat for the duration of the sea-trial and shall provide any necessary crew. The Buyer shall be entitled to be accompanied by up to two surveyors or advisers, any co-purchasers and not more than one member of his immediate family, subject to space constraints. The sea-trial shall take place in reasonable weather conditions and not more than five miles offshore. Unless agreed otherwise the Buyer and his party shall be responsible for supply of their own life jackets and other personal safety equipment. The Buyer shall be responsible for the cost of any fuel and oils consumed during the trials.

If, for any reason whatsoever the Boat has not performed to the Buyer's satisfaction on the sea-trial and he does not wish therefore to proceed with the purchase, he shall give written notice of his rejection of the boat to the seller within twenty four hours of the sea-trial or prior to the placing ashore of the boat for the inspection or survey referred to in Clause 5.2 below whichever shall be the sooner. In the event of the buyer giving notice of rejection, all fuel and oil expenses incurred by the seller on the sea-trial shall be payable by the buyer *from the deposit and the balance of the deposit shall be returned to the Buyer forthwith*. If notice of rejection is not given the sea-trial shall be deemed to have been to the Buyer's satisfaction.

The parties should discuss and agree the scope, range and form of the sea-trial in advance with each other and with any surveyor to avoid surprises or time wasting during the trial itself.

5.2 The Buyer may, at a venue to be agreed and at his own cost, slip or crane the boat ashore and open up the boat and her machinery for the purposes of inspection and/or survey which shall be completed within twenty one days of the signing of this agreement. If any inspection requires more than superficial non-destructive dismantling and limited removal of anti-fouling the consent of the Seller must be obtained before such work commences.

5.3 Within fourteen days of the completion of such inspection or survey (or receipt of any report, if later, thereon), if any material defect in the boat or her machinery, or any material deficiencies in her inventory have been found, other than any disclosed to the Buyer in writing prior to the signing of this agreement, the Buyer may:

EITHER

5.3.1

Give notice to the Seller of his rejection of the boat, provided that the notice shall specify the material defects or deficiencies. If the Buyer serves notice of rejection, then this agreement shall be deemed to be rescinded forthwith, *and the Seller shall refund the Deposit to the Buyer in accordance with Clause 8.*

OR

5.3.2

> Give notice to the Seller specifying all material defects or deficiencies mentioned in the report, and requiring the Seller either to make good the same, or make a sufficient reduction in the Purchase Price to enable the Buyer to make good the same. All required items of work to be completed without undue delay and carried out to meet the expressly specified requirements of the report. If the Buyer serves notice requiring the Seller to make good material defects or deficiencies, or to make a reduction in the Purchase Price, and the Seller has not agreed to make good such defects, or the Parties have not agreed a reduction in the Purchase Price within twenty one days, then this agreement shall be deemed to have been rescinded on the twenty second day after the service of notice, *and the Seller shall refund the Deposit to the Buyer in accordance with Clause 8.*

5.4 In the case of deficiencies in the boat's inventory remaining within seven days of acceptance in accordance with Clause 7, the deficiencies shall be made good or a reduction in the Purchase Price shall be agreed, failing which this Agreement shall be rescinded at the option of the Buyer only.

6.   Non-use by Seller:

The Seller agrees not to use the boat after completion of the survey undertaken on behalf of the Buyer except to move the boat to a suitable storage location and to conduct any sea-trials requested by the Buyer. If the boat is not accepted under the terms of this Agreement and the contract is rescinded, the Seller may thereafter use the boat.

7.   Acceptance of Boat or Rescission of Agreement

If the Buyer is using a solicitor or broker, the Seller should be informed and Clause 7 prefixed by words "Subject to the Buyer's inquiries as to the Seller's title".

7.1 The boat shall be deemed to have been accepted by the Buyer after the occurrence of any of the following events:

EITHER

7.1.1

The expiry of twenty two days from the date of this Agreement or such period as may be agreed in writing between the Parties, providing that no inspection or survey or arrangement for a sea trial has been commenced;

OR

7.1.2

The expiry of fifteen days from the completion of the inspection/ survey (or receipt of the written report by the Buyer) and/or sea trial or such extended period as may be agreed between the Parties, provided that the Buyer has not served notice under Clauses 5.3.1 or 5.3.2;

OR

7.1.3

The expiry of seven days, or such period as may be agreed between the Parties, from notification in writing by the Seller to the Buyer of completion of the remedial works specified in a notice given by the Buyer in Clause 5.3.2.

7.2 In the event of the rescission of this Agreement by the Buyer following inspection and/or survey, and/or sea-trial, he shall at his own expense reinstate the boat to the condition and position in which he found her, and shall pay all boatyard and surveyor's charges for this work, *and the Seller shall return the Deposit as specified under Clause 8.*

8.   Return of Deposit

Within seven days of the completion of any reinstatement work required under Clause 7.2, the Seller shall return the Deposit to the Buyer without deduction and without interest, save that he shall be entitled to retain such part of the Deposit necessary to defray any reasonable boatyard or surveyor's charges not paid by the Buyer. Neither Party shall thereafter have any claim against the other under this Agreement.

9. Risk

Until completion and delivery of the boat to the Buyer the boat shall be at the sole risk of the Seller who shall make good any damage sustained before actual delivery to the Buyer. If the boat becomes an actual or constructive loss before completion this Agreement shall terminate *and the Deposit shall be immediately returned to the Buyer without interest but without deduction or charge* and the Buyer shall have no claim against the Seller for damages. The Buyer shall, however, remain liable for the cost of any yard work or surveyor's fees commissioned by him or at his request. Upon delivery of the boat to the Buyer risk in the boat shall pass to the Buyer.

10. Completion/Title

Title in the boat shall pass to the Buyer upon completion in accordance with Clause 3.

11. Default by Buyer

Should the Buyer fail to pay the Purchase Price in accordance with Clause 3, the Seller may give notice in writing to the Buyer requiring him to complete the purchase within fourteen days of such notice. If the Buyer fails to comply with the notice then the Seller may re-sell the boat, and the Seller may claim from the Buyer the amount of any loss on re-sale, together with all his reasonable costs and expenses unless such default by the Buyer shall have arisen from events over which the Buyer had no control. *Any Deposit paid shall be forfeit provided that due allowance and refund to the Buyer shall be made if the Seller's loss, costs and expenses on the re-sale be less than the Deposit.*

12. Default by the Seller

If the Seller shall default in the execution of his part of the contract the Buyer shall, without prejudice to any other rights he may have, be entitled to *the return of the Deposit in full, without deduction, together with his reasonable costs, expenses and compensation for any loss which he may have sustained as a result of the Seller's default. Unless such default by the Seller shall have arisen from events over which the Seller had no control, the Seller shall pay interest upon the amount of the Deposit for the period during which he has held it at the rate of 4% per annum above Finance House base rate.*

13. Non-Production of Documents

The Seller has warranted that he is able to provide documentation as listed in the schedule to this Agreement. If the Seller is subsequently unable to provide the documentation as listed the Buyer shall be entitled to withdraw from this Agreement *and the Seller shall forthwith return the Deposit paid, if any, to the Buyer*.

If the Buyer shall have incurred the cost of a sea-trial and/or survey and is subsequently unable to continue with the purchase due to the Seller's inability to provide relevant documentation, the Buyer shall be at liberty to recover the cost of the sea-trial and/or survey and associated costs from the Seller.

14. Dispute Resolution

14.1

Disputes may, when they cannot be resolved by negotiation, with the written agreement of the Parties, be submitted to mediation.

14.2

Nothing in this clause shall affect the rights of the Parties to submit any dispute to the Courts of England & Wales, (or of Scotland if the Seller's address shall be in that country).

14.3

If any provision of this Agreement is held by any court or other competent authority to be void or unenforceable in whole or in part, this Agreement shall continue to be valid as to the other provisions thereof and the remainder of the affected provision.

15. Notices

Any notice to the Buyer or Seller under this Agreement shall be in writing and shall be sufficiently served if delivered to him personally, faxed, or posted by recorded delivery to the address set out in this Agreement. Any notice posted shall be deemed to have been received two days after the time of posting, and any notice delivered personally or by fax shall be deemed to have been received from the time of delivery.

16. Law

This agreement shall be governed by the law of England and Wales (or of Scotland if the Seller's address shall be in that country) and the Parties agree to submit to the jurisdiction of the courts of those countries.

17. Marginal Notes

The construction of this Agreement is not to be affected by any marginal notes.

18. Entire Agreement

This agreement together with any schedule and/or inventory signed by both Seller and Buyer forms the entire agreement between the Parties unless otherwise specifically agreed in writing between them.

19. Third Party Rights

For the purpose of the Contracts (Rights of Third Parties) Act 1999, this agreement does not and is not intended to give any rights to enforce any of its provisions, to any person who is not a Party to it.

SIGNED BY THE SELLER(S):

In the presence of: (Witness signature)

(Witness full name and address)

If the boat is jointly owned, then all owners to sign as joint Sellers.

SIGNED BY THE BUYER(S):

In the presence of: (Witness signature)

(Witness full name and address)

If the boat is being jointly purchased, then all Buyers to sign as joint Buyers.

INVENTORY: **(See Clause 1)**

SCHEDULE OF DOCUMENTS (See Clauses 3.1.1/3.1.2)

The following documents should normally be available; however the Parties may agree to delete some of them, or to include others. Any deletions or additions should be initialled by the Parties.

1. All Certificates of Registry in the Seller's possession relating to the boat current or expired;

2. A properly executed Bill of Sale in a form to be approved by the Buyer in favour of the Seller;

3. Bills of Sale tracing ownership from the very first owner of the vessel to the current Seller;

4. Builder's certificate;

5. Builder's invoices;

6. Original/copy (receipted) VAT invoice;

7. Evidence of date of arrival in the European Community;

8. Confirmation of RCD compliance in the form of an owner's manual (including or together with a written declaration of conformity) or details of RCD exemption;

9. Any other documents in the Seller's possession relating to his acquisition of the vessel, which may include:

   a. Equipment manuals;

   b. Service records;

   c. Receipts for repair work;

   d. Racing Certificates;

   e. Mooring charges;

   f. Harbour dues.

10. Where the Seller is a company, certified copies of the corporate authorities approving this agreement and appointing the signatories for the Bill of Sale;

11. Any delivery order or authority necessary to enable the Buyer to take immediate possession of the boat.

APPENDIX 2

AGREEMENT FOR THE SYNDICATE OWNERSHIP OF A BOAT

Name of Boat:

Flag and Port of Registry (if any):

Lying at:

Register Status: (Part I/Part III/Other/Unregistered)

Official No: **HIN/CIN Number:**

Principal Dimensions:

Hull Length Overall: **Beam:**   **Draught:**

Gross Registered Tonnage:

Engines (make, power and date of build):

Description and Construction Materials:

Builder:

Date of Build:

Date of Purchase by Seller:

Financed   **YES/NO**   **By:**

Amount of Finance Outstanding at Date of Agreement:

VAT Paid in EU?   **YES/NO**

AN AGREEMENT made the   day of   20   .

BETWEEN   of

                                      ('the first owner').

and   of

                                      ('the second owner').

[The number of owners can be increased according to the current and proposed ownership of the boat.]

The owners include their respective successors in title and shall hereinafter be collectively referred to as 'the Parties'.

WHEREAS the Parties wish to enter into an agreement to share the management and use of the boat " 	"

('the Boat').

[and **WHEREAS** the first owner is the present owner of the Boat and **WHEREAS** the second owner has by a prior contract purchased from the first owner 	/64ths of the Boat]

[and **WHEREAS** the Parties have purchased the Boat as [co-owners in the following shares:

the first owner purchasing 	/64ths

the second owner purchasing 	/64ths]; or

as joint owners]

[and **WHEREAS** the Parties have [jointly and severally] entered into an agreement with [	] (the "Mortgage Company")].

NOW IT IS HEREBY MUTUALLY AGREED between the Parties as follows:

1.   Joint Bank Account

The first owner shall forthwith open a [Bank/Building Society] account ("the Account") in the names of the Parties into which the Parties shall upon the [   ] day of [   ] in each year transfer the amount of £[   ] until six months after the termination of this agreement in accordance with Clause 5.

2.   Withdrawals and Contributions from/to Account

The [first] [and second] owner(s) shall have power [jointly/ separately] to draw monies from the Account for the sole purpose of the maintenance and management of the Boat as [he/they] shall in their absolute discretion think fit and shall have power to call for further and necessary contributions in equal shares from [the second owner/each other] subject always to the safeguards in Clause 4.7 and to the general law affecting principal and agent.

3. Casual Disbursements

Any disbursement, payment or account discharged by one owner on behalf of the other and of the general management of the Boat shall from time to time as convenient but certainly once annually be reported to the other owner and each owner [jointly and severally] agrees to contribute [one half] of such disbursements, payments or accounts upon proper documentation in the form of receipts, etc. being presented as evidence of payment.

4. Management responsibility

The [first] owner shall have the following powers, duties and responsibilities:

4.1 to make day-to-day decisions for the general management of the Boat;

4.2 to make (after consultation with the [second] owner(s)) any arrangement for the purchase of capital equipment such as sails, engines, etc. as may be necessary and for any agreement to charter the Boat;

4.3 to insure the Boat, her apparel, fittings etc. against the usual risks with a marine insurance company or association;

4.4 to employ any yard, sail-loft, brokers or agents on their usual terms of business and to transact any necessary business in relation to the Boat;

4.5 to make, adjust, apportion or settle at his discretion any salvage, damage, average or other claims in favour of or against the Boat or to refer the same to mediation or arbitration;

4.6 to take such steps as may be necessary to defend proceedings, accept service or arrange finance relating to the Boat;

4.7 as soon as reasonably practicable after the [   ] day of [   ] in each year to render to the [second] owner accounts paid together with the Account statements as evidence of payment, and on request to produce all vouchers, books or other documents and papers relating to the management of the Account and of the Boat.

5. Termination of Agreement

5.1 If either of the Parties has reasonable cause or desire to sell his share in the Boat and thereby terminate this agreement, he may, by individual notice in writing to the other Party, indicate his desire to sell and terminate. Such sale and termination shall take place within six months after the delivery of such notice in writing.

5.2 Upon such notice in writing being delivered, the remaining Parties shall take such steps as may be necessary to secure the execution of a proper release and indemnity against all liabilities contracted by the determining Party and shall arrange to purchase the share of the determining Party at a fair market price or alternatively the determining Party and the remaining Parties shall obtain agreement by another to take on the share of the determining Party. Where another takes on the share of the determining Party it shall be the responsibility of the determining party to pay for any advertising or other such expenses incurred in relation to the sale. The determining Party hereby agrees to defray or settle his share of the disbursements, payments or accounts for the Boat up to and including the date of actual termination as agreed between the Parties which for the avoidance of doubt may be any date within six months of the individual notice in writing being received by the other Party.

5.3 If a dispute arises as to the price to be paid to the determining Party for his share then a valuation shall be obtained from a recognised yacht broker or surveyor and in default of agreement then the entirety of the Boat shall be publicly advertised for sale with notice of time and place for sale being given to both Parties and she shall be sold. Each of the Parties on receiving his share of the purchase money shall execute the necessary Bill of Sale of his share in the Boat to the purchaser and deliver up possession of the Boat. The costs of such sale shall be paid by the Parties according to their respective shares.

5.4 Where it is agreed to terminate this agreement and the Parties have mutually agreed to sell the Boat, it shall then be sold either by private treaty at such price as the Parties may agree or, in default of such agreement, by public auction subject to such conditions as are usual on the sale of such boats. Each of the

Parties shall be at liberty to bid for and purchase the Boat at any such public auction, or to purchase the Boat outright for the price advertised for sale by private treaty.

5.5 In the event of the death of one of the Parties the Deceased's share of the Boat shall pass in accordance with the Deceased's Will or the Intestate Rules. If the Beneficiary of the Deceased Party's share elects to sell his share in the Boat he shall do so in accordance with Clause 5 of this Agreement.

6. *Regular payment of mortgage etc.*

In the case of a mortgage or hire purchase agreement being in operation each owner [jointly and severally] agrees to pay his monthly or other contribution to defray the costs of such mortgage or hire purchase agreement into the Account in accordance with Clause 1 until the date of determination agreed in accordance with Clause 5.

7. *Final settlement of Mortgage Debt*

In the event of the sale of the Boat, each owner [jointly and severally] agrees with the other to defray from his share of the sale price his share of the mortgage or hire purchase agreement entered into with the Mortgage Company.

8. *Dispute Resolution*

Disputes may, when they cannot be resolved by negotiation, with the written agreement of the Parties, be submitted to mediation.

Nothing in this clause shall affect the rights of the Parties to submit any dispute to the Courts of England & Wales, (or of Scotland if the first owner's address shall be in that country).

9. *Notices*

Any notice under this agreement shall be in writing and shall be sufficiently served if delivered personally, faxed or posted to the address set out in this agreement. Any notice posted shall be deemed to have been received two days after the time of posting, and any notice delivered personally or by fax shall be deemed to have been received from the time of delivery.

10. Law

This agreement shall be governed by the law of England and Wales (or of Scotland if the first owner's address shall be in that country) and the Parties agree to submit to the jurisdiction of the courts of those countries.

11. Marginal Notes

The construction of this agreement is not to be affected by any marginal notes.

12. Third Party Rights

For the purpose of the Contract (Rights of Third Parties) Act 1999, this agreement does not and is not intended to give any rights to enforce any of its provisions, to any person who is not a Party to it.

IN WITNESS whereof this agreement has been signed by the Parties the day and year first above written

SIGNED BY THE FIRST OWNER..

in the presence of:

SIGNED BY THE SECOND OWNER..

in the presence of:

APPENDIX 3

ABYA CODE OF PRACTICE - NOVEMBER 2005 EDITION

Terminology: 'Brokers' sell second-hand boats on behalf of the owner.

'Yacht Agents' includes all new boat sales personnel, dealers and distributors and part exchange sales.

1. Introduction

The Yacht Brokers, Designers and Surveyors Association was originally set up in 1912, and has steadily enlarged and enhanced its operations since then.

The Yacht Brokers, Designers and Surveyors Association is the holding company for two individual and independent Associations, the Association of Brokers and Yacht Agents ("ABYA") and the Yacht Designers & Surveyors Association ("YDSA"). The individual Associations have separate committees and manage their affairs individually but administration is handled by the YBDSA secretariat.

ABYA exists to promote the highest standards of professionalism and expert knowledge in the field of yacht sales, and expects high standards of its members. Membership is only open to existing practising brokers and new boat sales personnel with a proven track record in the industry. For all grades of membership there is rigorous scrutiny of the applicant's work. A Continuous Professional Development scheme exists to ensure that members update their knowledge regularly, and Members' work is monitored on a regular basis. The Association holds regular training Seminars and Forums in house and maintains close contact with other professionals in the marine industry such as Law firms and Insurance houses, many of whom are "**Subscribers**" to the Association. All members are required to carry Professional Indemnity insurance.

Grades of Membership

Associate Member - The entry grade of membership. Those who undertake the ABYA "Introduction to Brokerage" course receive automatic Associate membership, free for the first year, provided they are working in brokerage and hold appropriate PI insurance. They will be invited to remain as members at the end of the year, at the currently applicable membership fee. Associates should not generally remain at this grade for more than three years. Applicants who have not undertaken the course but can show evidence of their experience by submission of documentation, 2 professional references and evidence of holding appropriate PI may also be admitted as Associate Members.

Associate Members may apply to up-grade once they have been engaged in boat sales continuously for at least three years immediately preceding the application.

A **Full Member** is a member who has been an Associate Broker Member for a continuous period of at least three years and has during such period been actively engaged as a principal or Senior Broker and who, in the opinion of the Committee, has gained a good reputation, is capable of acting in his own right in conducting business, and is capable of dealing with yachts and small craft of various types and materials. Experienced brokers or new boat sales people may apply to enter directly as Full Members. If the applicant has not been a member for three years or at all but has been actively engaged as principal for a continuous period of ten years the Committee may admit him as a member on account of his outstanding achievements.

There are also "**Fellow**" and "**Honorary**" grades of membership, granted by the Association in recognition of exceptional services to the Association or the profession.

Members are encouraged to use the ABYA logo and letters "ABYA" on their stationery and advertising. Electronic versions are available from the secretariat.

2   Preamble

Every Broker or New Boat Sales Member of the Association shall observe this Code of Conduct in line with the Memorandum and Articles of Association of the ABYA and YBDSA. ("Member" includes Associate, Full, Fellow and Honorary Members).

It should be noted that there are local variations to practices, particularly on the inland waterways.

The use of the masculine is intended to include any ABYA Member, male or female.

The purpose of this code is to define the rules of professional conduct to be followed by all Members of the YBDSA, whose sub-association is the Association of Brokers and Yacht Agents (ABYA).

The YBDSA and ABYA shall not be held responsible in any way for any work undertaken by any Member whether in compliance with the Code of Conduct or outside its guidelines.

3   Types of service that may be offered

- New boat sales

- Brokerage on second-hand boats

- Part Exchange

- British Registration

- Checking of Legal Title

- Checking compliance with the Recreational Craft Directive (RCD)

- Tonnage Measurement Surveys

- Checking VAT status of the vessel

- Bill of Sale

- Assisting with arrangement of finance

3.1 The ABYA Member shall ensure he is correctly registered under the FSA regulations if he is offering and arranging finance, and registered as a High Value Dealer if he takes, or is likely to take, cash payments at any time.

3.2 The Member shall set up a Client Account, designated as such, and identified at the Bank as such, where he shall hold all client monies, as these monies are held in trust for the client and are not to be used for company purposes.

3.3 The Member who sells boats as Part Exchange shall be aware of his responsibilities and shall ensure that he has good title to pass to the purchaser. As a commercial vendor he is bound by the terms of the Sale of Goods Acts including, *inter alia*, that the goods shall be fit for the purpose. In the case of a defect being found, the burden of proof for the 6 months after the sale is on the seller to prove the defect was absent at the time of the sale; thereafter it is for the purchaser to prove that it was.

4 *Professional Conduct*

4.1 ABYA Members shall discharge their professional responsibilities with integrity and shall at all times act and report in a fair and factual manner. They shall be independent of all other parties unless working in conjunction with another sales company.

4.2 ABYA Members should acquaint themselves with the ABYA Guidance Notes and abide by these notes in their dealings.

4.3 Members should acquaint themselves with the Memorandum and Articles of Association of ABYA and of YBDSA (Holdings) Ltd.

4.4 Professional advice is confidential to the instructing Client and may normally only be disclosed to a third party with the express permission of that Client.

4.5 They shall not offer any hidden benefit to any third party. No ABYA Member who is acting on behalf of a client shall accept any hidden benefit from any party to the sale.

4.6 If a Member knowingly has, once had or acquires in the future, a financial or other vested interest in a vessel, product or service which he has been asked to offer for sale, he shall declare that interest to his Client, either at the time or at any future time when the member first becomes aware of such an interest.

4.7 An ABYA Member is not empowered to commission work on a vessel without prior instructions from the owner or his representative.

4.8 An ABYA Member acting as an independent consultant should disclose any possible conflict of interest and should not undertake work where his independence could be influenced in any way which would affect his obligation to the instructing Client.

4.9 An ABYA Member should at all times present a fair, objective, and unbiased opinion on the potential market value of the vessel, maintaining his independence and impartiality at all times.

4.10

An ABYA Member should act at all times with impartiality with respect to creed, gender, nationality or disability of the persons he is dealing with.

4.11

The Client should be advised at the time of listing of the vessel of the amount of the commission or other fees and any additional expenses to be charged and whether VAT is payable.

4.12

The Member is strongly encouraged to use a written Listing Agreement when taking instructions from the client before offering the vessel for sale. He should also prepare a detailed inventory of the vessel to be offered for sale and agree this with the client for the avoidance of doubt at a later date. The inventory should include the following items that are to be left (as applicable):

- All mechanical, electrical and electronic equipment

- Any sails (if applicable)

- Liferaft

- Tender

- Anchor(s)

- Spare warps etc.

- Fenders

- Charts

- Owners Manual

- Technical Manual

- Any soft furnishings

- Other removable objects

4.13

The Member should ascertain and, if possible, obtain at an early stage from the vendor the documentation he has available to prove title, compliance with the RCD (if necessary), evidence of VAT payment (or similar payment within the EU), or VAT exemption, Registration, outstanding finance, Bills of Sale from previous owners and the Builder's Certificate. A new Bill of Sale from the current owner to the new owner must be completed and passed with all documentation pertaining to the vessel to the new owner on completion.

4.14

The Member shall provide a written Sale & Purchase Agreement as between the two parties which should be signed by both parties. Any amendments shall be agreed and initialled by both parties. This should be done at an early stage and include any deposit payment, and other terms relating to the timescale for survey, sea-trial, etc. to ensure there is no misunderstanding at a later stage. NB: variations on the process on the inland waterways.

4.15

The Member shall check as far as he is able whether there are any outstanding mortgages, liens or bills relating to the vessel (e.g. mooring fees, chandlery bills) and should settle these from the completion monies before sending the balance to the vendor.

4.16

The Member shall send the balance of the completion monies to the vendor as soon as is practicable, once all the paperwork has been completed.

5   Complaints Procedure

5.1 If a Client has a matter of concern in respect of the service he has received, he should initially take this up with the Member concerned, so that he may have the opportunity to clarify the situation or suggest a remedy, etc.

5.2 If the Client is not satisfied they may then notify the matter to ABYA – (providing the broker or sales person is a member) who will refer the matter to their Disciplinary Sub-Committee for consideration if it is thought to be a matter of professional misconduct. This sub-committee comprises senior members of the Association who are experienced in boat sales matters. A "Complaints Protocol" form will be sent out to all complainants setting out the information required before the committee can meet to decide on the issue.

5.3 The disciplinary sub-committee will make a judgement based on the information supplied to them at the outset. Once this decision has been made there will be no scope for further discussion. It is therefore highly important that all the relevant evidence is supplied at the outset.

5.4 Sanctions may be applied to the Member by the Disciplinary Sub-Committee if appropriate including one or more of the following:

- Calling the member for interview so that he may state his case to senior Company members;

- Removal from the Company's web site members' listing and from any other publications produced by the Company (which may be rescinded by agreement of Committee at a later date);

- Demotion by a grade of membership (which may be rescinded by agreement of Committee at a later date);

- Suspension (which may be lifted by agreement of Committee at a later date);

- Expulsion of such member.

5.5 The Association will use its best endeavours to achieve a resolution on behalf of their member and the Client, but cannot become a party to the proceedings.

5.6 Note that for matters which are the subject of a potential or actual technical complaint and which may proceed to law, the matter is potentially *sub-judice* and the sub-committee may not take any further action until it is resolved and they may investigate any possible contravention of the rules of the Association.

5.7 Should a resolution not be achieved, the matter may be referred to arbitration or conciliation, subject to the agreement of the two parties, the choice of arbitrator to be similarly agreed.

5.8 Clients should be aware that the Member is required to advise his Professional Indemnity Insurers immediately on notification of any matter which may become the subject of a claim and may not thereafter be permitted by his insurers to enter into direct correspondence with the client.

APPENDIX 4

Marine Finance Houses in BMF Membership

1. Lombard Marine Finance
PO Box 464, Templars Way
Chandlers Ford, Eastleigh SO53 3US

Tel: 023 8024 2171

2. Barclays Marine Finance
The Chandlery Building
Offices 3 & 4 1st Floor
Hamble Point Marina
School Lane, Hamble
Southampton SO31 4NB

Tel: 0800 445644

3. Bank of Scotland Marine
1st Floor, Jellicoe House
Botleigh Grange, Hedge End
Southampton SO30 2AF

Tel: 0845 603 2362

4. HSBC Marine Finance
PO Box 4496, 12 Calthorpe Road
Edgbaston, Birmingham BH15 1HS

Tel: 0845 607 6007

APPENDIX 5

Bill of Sale

FOR THE BOAT   ....('the Boat')

Type: ....
Year built: ....
Length: ....
Beam: ....
Auxiliary Power: ....
Small Ships Reg. No: ....
Hull/Craft Identification Number ....
Lying at   ....

I/we   .... [and   ....
of: .... of: ....
         ....]
am/are the legal *[joint] owner(s) of the Boat ([together] 'the
Transferor[s]'). The Transferor(s) has/have agreed to the transfer of
the Boat to:

         .... [and   ....
of: .... of: ....
         ....]

IN CONSIDERATION of the sum of £.........................

(................................ pounds) paid to me/us by the Transferee(s)
receipt of which is acknowledged; the Transferor(s) hereby:

1. **Transfer the Boat to the Transferee[s];**
2. For myself/ourselves and for my/our heirs **covenant** with the
Transferee[s] and his/their heirs and assigns that I/we have power so
to transfer and that the Boat is free from encumbrances.

SIGNED this.........................day of .... 20[   ]

....   (signature of Transferor[s])
[........................]

in the presence of:
         .... (signature of Witness)
         .... (name of Witness)
of: .... (address of Witness)

Notes:

1. This form of Bill of Sale is produced by the RYA for use by personal members for the transfer of an unregistered boat or a boat registered on the Part III (Small Ships) Register. Transfers of boats registered under Part I of the Central Register of British Ships should be evidenced using the Bill of Sale prescribed by the Maritime and Coastguard Agency obtainable from the UK Ship Register (RSS).

    In order to re-register or de-register your boat, please contact the UK Ship Register (RSS), PO Box 420, Cardiff, CF24 5XR. Tel. 02920 448800.

2. * Please delete as applicable.

3. This form of Bill of Sale should not be used when transfer is by gift, or if any of the parties to it is a corporate body.

4. "Joint" ownership is where two or more people all own the whole boat. "Co-ownership" is where two or more people each own a proportion (i.e. share) of the boat. This distinction may be significant, for example, if one owner were to die. If the deceased were a joint owner, ownership of the whole boat would automatically pass to the surviving owner(s). If the deceased owner were a co-owner then their share would form part of their estate and would be disposed of accordingly. If the Transferor(s) or Transferee(s) are joint owners then no figure should be inserted for the percentage share held by each.
    More information on joint and co-ownership can be found in the RYA leaflet "Joint Ownership or Co-Ownership".

5. Where the Transferees intend to hold the legal title to the boat as co-owners they will need to use a Syndicate Bill of Sale and they may therefore wish obtain a copy of the RYA's Syndicate Pack.

APPENDIX 6

Taxation rates in EU states as at July 2009

AUSTRIA	VAT at 20%
BELGIUM	VAT 21% on new or imported boats. "First Registration" tax of 25M ECU payable on new boats above 7.5m. Registration tax of 2500 ECU decreasing by 10% per annum payable on resale.
BULGARIA	VAT at 20%
CYPRUS	VAT at 15%
CZECH REPUBLIC	VAT at 19%
DENMARK	VAT payable on full value of boat when dealer is involved in transaction in force. VAT rate 25%. Light and navaid tax based on 1% of insurance value in force.
ESTONIA	VAT at 20%
FINLAND	VAT at 22%.
FRANCE	VAT at 19.6%. Tax on all users of inland waterways under consideration. Annual user tax based on engine power greater than 5hp and hull size (greater than 3GRT) in force.
GERMANY	Tax on dealer's margin in force. VAT on new boats 19% in force.

GREECE	VAT at 19%
HUNGARY	VAT at 25%
IRELAND	VAT at 21.5%
ITALY	VAT at 20%
LATVIA	VAT at 21%
LITHUANIA	VAT at 21%
LUXEMBOURG	VAT at 15%
MALTA	VAT at 18%
NETHERLANDS	VAT at 19%
POLAND	VAT at 22%
PORTUGAL	VAT at 20% for all types of boats. Annual tax depending on length and engine power.
ROMANIA	VAT at 19%
SLOVAKIA	VAT at 19%
SLOVENIA	VAT at 20%
SPAIN	VAT at 16% on all boats plus a 13% registration tax on boats over 7.5m. This is compulsory for Spanish nationals and to all others who wish to register their boat in Spain.
SWEDEN	VAT at 25%
UK	VAT at 17.5% from 1/1/2010

APPENDIX 7

Useful Contacts

Royal Yachting Association
RYA House, Ensign Way
Hamble, Southampton
SO31 4YA

Tel: 0845 345 0400
www.rya.org.uk

British Marine Federation
Marine House
Thorpe Lea Road, Egham
Surrey TW20 8BF

Tel: 01784 473377
www.britishmarine.co.uk

UK Ship Register
Registry of Shipping and Seamen
P.O. Box 420
Cardiff CF24 5XR

Tel: 02920 448800
www.ukshipregister.co.uk

Yacht Brokers, Designers and Surveyors Association
The Glass Works
Penns Road
Petersfield, Hampshire
GU32 2EW

Tel: 01730 710425
www.ybdsa.co.uk

HM Revenue & Customs

VAT National Advice Service 0845 010 9000
www.hmrc.gov.uk

APPENDIX 8

Notice 8 - Extract Deemed VAT Paid Status

Certain vessels that were in use as private pleasure craft prior to 1 January 1985 and were in the EU on 31 December 1992, may be deemed VAT paid under the Single Market transitional arrangements. As Austria, Finland and Sweden joined the EU later, the relevant dates for vessels in these countries are 'in use' before 1 January 1987 and moored in EU on 31 December 1994.

The following documents are useful to prove the age and location of the vessel:

For Age	For Location
Marine survey	Receipt for mooring
Part 1 Registration	Receipt for harbour dues
Insurance documents	Dry dock records
Builder's certificate	

If you are unable to provide any of the above, whilst cruising within the EU you should carry a Bill of Sale (between two private individuals in the UK). Whilst this is not conclusive proof that VAT has been paid, it does indicate that tax status is the responsibility of UK Customs. It is also advisable to contact the relevant authorities in the Member State, or their Embassy in the UK, to confirm what documentation will be required in advance of your voyage.

APPENDIX 9

*Normal order of events for the private purchase of a
secondhand boat*

- See boat and make offer subject to contract and survey.

- Consider how best to protect your purchase monies; if buying
  through a broker make enquiries of its use of a client account.

- Pay deposit and receive a receipt and signed Sale Agreement in
  return (which should include a signed inventory of the boat's
  machinery, equipment and gear to be included in the sale),
  agree dates for completion.

- Ask for proof of ownership before paying for a survey/sea-trial.

- Ask whether there is marine finance on the boat and if so
  establish the arrangements for discharge prior to completion.

- Ask for confirmation of Recreational Craft Directive compliance
  or exemption and VAT status of the boat.

- Instruct surveyor.

- Await his report.

- Negotiate on work to rectify material defects, agree adjusted
  price if necessary.

- Ask to see all equipment and gear which is not currently on the
  boat but which is included in the inventory prior to handing over
  the balance of the purchase price.

- Arrange insurance prior to handing over balance cheque.

- On handing over balance make sure you receive Bill of Sale,
  previous Bills of Sale if possible, Certificate of Registration or
  letters or Statutory Declarations from previous owners
  relinquishing further interest in the boat, Builder's Certificate,
  Original/copy (receipted) VAT invoice RCD compliance and all
  other relevant documentation.

INDEX

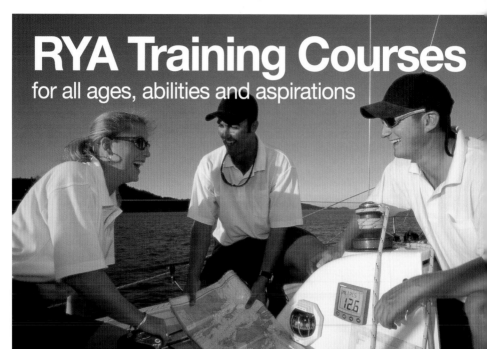

RYA Membership

Promoting and Protecting Boating

The RYA is the national organisation which represents the interests of everyone who goes boating for pleasure.

The greater the membership, the louder our voice when it comes to protecting members' interests.

Apply for membership today, and support the RYA, to help the RYA support you.

Benefits of Membership

- Special members' discounts on a range of products and services including boat insurance, books, charts, DVD's and class certificates

- Access to expert advice on all aspects of boating from legal wrangles to training matters

- Free issue of Certificates of Competence, increasingly asked for by everyone from overseas governments to holiday companies, insurance underwriters to boat hirers

- Access to the wide range of RYA publications, including the quarterly magazine

- Third Party insurance for windsurfing members

- Free Internet access with RYA-On-line

- Special discounts on AA membership

- Regular offers in RYA Magazine

- ...and much more

JOIN NOW

Membership form opposite or join online at *www.rya.org.uk*

Visit our website for information, advice, members' services and web shop.

IT'S ALL ABOUT YOU AND THE BOATING YOU DO

RYA MEMBERSHIP APPLICATION

One of boating's biggest attractions is its freedom from rules and regulations. As an RYA member you'll play an active part in keeping it that way, as well as benefiting from free expert advice and information, plus discounts on a wide range of boating products, charts and publications.

To join the RYA, please complete the application form below and send it to The Membership Department, RYA, RYA House, Ensign Way, Hamble, Southampton, Hampshire SO31 4YA. You can also join online at www.rya.org.uk, or by phoning the membership department on +44 (0) 23 8060 4159. Whichever way you choose to apply, you can save money by paying by Direct Debit. A Direct Debit instruction is on the back of this form.

RYA
Be part of it

	Title	Forename	Surname	Gender	Date of Birth
Applicant ❶					D D / M M / Y Y Y Y
Applicant ❷					D D / M M / Y Y Y Y
Applicant ❸					D D / M M / Y Y Y Y
Applicant ❹					D D / M M / Y Y Y Y

Address

Post Code

E-mail Applicant ❶
E-mail Applicant ❷
E-mail Applicant ❸
E-mail Applicant ❹

Home Tel   Day Time Tel   Mobile Tel

Type of membership required (Tick Box)

Junior (0-11)	Annual rate £5 or **£5** if paying by Direct Debit
Youth (12-17)	Annual rate £14 or **£11** if paying by Direct Debit
Under 25	Annual rate £22 or **£22** if paying by Direct Debit
Personal	Annual rate £43 or **£39** if paying by Direct Debit
Family*	Annual rate £63 or **£59** if paying by Direct Debit

Save money by completing the Direct Debit form overleaf

Please number up to three boating interests in order, with number one being your principal interest

Yacht Racing	Yacht Cruising	Dinghy Racing	Dinghy Cruising
Personal Watercraft	Sportboats & RIBs	Windsurfing	Motor Boating
Powerboat Racing	Canal Cruising	River Cruising	

* *Family Membership: 2 adults plus any under 18s all living at the same address. Prices valid until 30/9/2011. One discount voucher is accepted for individual memberships, and two discount vouchers are accepted for family membership.*

IMPORTANT In order to provide you with membership benefits the details provided by you on this form and in the course of your membership will be maintained on a database.

If you do not wish to receive information on member services and benefits please tick here ☐ By applying for membership of the RYA you agree to be bound by the RYA's standard terms and conditions (copies on request or at www.rya.org.uk)

Signature

Date   D D / M M / Y Y Y Y

Source Code

Joining Point Code

RYA
Be part of it

GET MORE FROM
YOUR
BOATING
SUPPORT THE
RYA

PAY BY DIRECT DEBIT – AND SAVE MONEY

Instructions to your Bank or Building Society to pay by Direct Debit

Please fill in the form and send to:
Membership Department, Royal Yachting Association, RYA House, Ensign Way, Hamble,
Southampton, Hampshire SO31 4YA.

DIRECT Debit

Name and full postal address of your Bank/Building Society

To the Manager   Bank/Building Society

Address

                        Postcode

Name(s) of Account Holder(s)

Branch Sort Code

Bank/Building Society Account Number

Originator's Identification Number

| 9 | 5 | 5 | 2 | 1 | 3 |

RYA Membership Number (For office use only)

Instructions to your Bank or Building Society

Please pay Royal Yachting Association Direct Debits from the account detailed in
this instruction subject to the safeguards assured by The Direct Debit Guarantee.
I understand that this instruction may remain with the Royal Yachting Association
and, if so, details will be passed electronically to my Bank/Building Society.

Signature(s)

Date: D D / M M / Y Y Y Y